Done With Work:
A Dozen Perspectives
On The Decision To Retire

Larry Gard, Ph.D.

DEDICATION

To GSC, with thanks for your boundless love, enthusiasm, and support.

CONTENTS

FOREWORD

Retirement creates an unnatural life sequence. Throughout our lives most events proceed in order, from beginning to middle to end. But by its very nature, retiring changes the normal flow. Retirement starts with the *ending* of the life you experienced for decades, and moves toward the *beginning* of a new life after leaving your current position.

Dr. Gard's book provides insights and personal examples of how you can make a successful transition between the "Ending" of what you have been doing for decades and the "Beginning" of the next stage of your life. As the founder and CEO of the Successful Transition Planning Institute, I highly suggest that you spend your time reading this book since it will help prepare you to move into a new life of meaning and purpose.

One of the many things that I found effective about this book is Larry's decision to interview people who have, or are in the process of retiring, which positions them as reliable sources regarding transitioning. Their stories help you become aware of what has worked with people who have retired and also what did not work during the retirement process. This knowledge can help you avoid making the same mistakes.

Done With Work also reinforces the important concept that you must *know who* you really are in order to *know what* you really want to do in the next chapter of your life. Taking the time to identify and clarify your values at this stage of your life enables you to find outlets to express them. The book helps you answer, "who am I?" when you are no longer a player and the person that people turn to for professional answers.

Larry's interviews provide a unique perspective by capturing the decision-making process of people who chose to retire from their full-time positions and the resulting mental shift that occurs. A number of people interviewed expressed how retirement brought them freedom from career responsibilities, but also made them responsible for creating a new structure for their lives. A common theme that emerged was the importance of having a sense of purpose and taking the time to apply the power of intentionality to create a plan for their lives. Many people interviewed for this book expressed that the loss of their personal and professional identities was a major issue during the process of retiring. A common theme for many of the people who Larry interviewed was the importance of having a clear direction as they entered into the next stage of their lives. Also, finding meaningful activities was a key element in creating a fulfilling retirement.

Larry brings a unique integrated perspective to the consideration of retiring by looking at both the internal psychological factors as well as the external circumstances that can be involved in the retirement decision. I found Larry's professional observations at the end of each interview enlightening and the concluding chapter of the book insightful. Larry's counseling experience and practical understanding will help people make successful transitions into the next stage of their lives. I highly recommend this book.

Jack Beauregard
Founder and CEO
Successful Transition Planning Institute
Cambridge, MA

ACKNOWLEDGMENTS

My sincere thanks to those who participated in the interviews for this book. Your willingness to give of your time, your ability to reflect on your decision-making process, and your unbridled candor is deeply appreciated.

My gratitude to Ali, Bruce, Cathy, David, Gail, Janine, Kieran, and Ron for your help in identifying people to share their stories. Sadly, I cannot mention your last names because doing so could potentially compromise the anonymity of those interviewed.

Special thanks to Bruce Stevens for his thoughtful editorial advice, and to Denada Hoxha, Ph.D. for helping me stay focused and committed to this project.

Chapter 1
Introduction

For Americans in good health, retirement could possibly be the longest phase of their lives, far longer than adolescence. But quite frankly most of us don't spend much time thinking about it. We do little to prepare ourselves from an emotional standpoint and the guidance we get can often be summed up as: "Save more than you think you'll need, and try to remain active." Wise notions perhaps, but not sufficient to help us navigate through and beyond a major life transition.

To some extent not wanting to think about the future may even be linked to our language. Yale economist Keith Chen has studied how a person's language can subtly affect their propensity to save for the future. Speakers of languages that grammatically separate the future from the present (including US English) save less and retire with less wealth. But no matter what language we speak, retirement awaits millions of baby boomers whether we want to think about it or not. According to numbers compiled by the Pew Research Center and the Social Security Administration roughly 10,000 baby boomers retire every single day.

Deciding to retire usually involves thinking about what comes next. Without the structure and demands of work, life in retirement can present a seemingly blank canvas. There are days, weeks, months, and years waiting to be etched with meaningful experiences and satisfying time spent. How will you fill all of this time?

Advertisements and the popular media offer us some attractive notions. We typically see happy older couples posing onboard a cruise ship, biking down a leafy lane, kayaking through a scenic bay, or driving along a coastal road in a convertible. Although these idealized scenes are appealing, they don't represent the day-to-day experience of most people. Even those retirees who have the good fortune to enjoy frequent travel and recreation still have to come home eventually, if only to plan their next adventure!

Some people I've met describe the prospect of retirement as something akin to jumping off a proverbial cliff of uncertainty. They don't have a clue about what they will do when they stop working and this creates great uneasiness. Some fear that they will become bored or that they will regret their decision to retire. Others, having watched a parent or grandparent suffer in retirement, fear that their experience will be unpleasant as well. And still others worry that they will feel diminished and adrift without the sense of personal identity they derive from work.

Given the magnitude of the uncertainty and unease, it is understandable why some people resist retirement. In some cases they continue working despite compelling evidence that doing so is counterproductive. Others retire, but do so with unconsidered or unrealistic ideas about how to spend their time, only to feel within a year the exact discontent they dreaded.

Even if you think long and hard about your post retirement life, you're facing some pretty big questions:

- Have you accomplished professionally what you had hoped to? If not, can you accept what remains unfinished?

- How do you imagine other people will think about you and treat you once they find out you've retired and/or sold your business?

- How will you structure your time? Will you need to have a new routine in place immediately or will you be comfortable allowing one to emerge gradually?

- What are your assumptions and beliefs? What do you anticipate will happen once you decide to stop working? Are you making assumptions that may not be warranted?

- How will your roles change once you leave work? How will it feel to relinquish some of those roles, and what new ones might you take on?

- Can you tolerate not being involved in business decisions, not being in the loop, etc.?

The Decision to Be Done

The more I thought about retirement and how people construct their post-work lives, the more curious I became about how people make the decision to retire in the first place. Of course some people don't have much choice. They work in settings that have clear, defined, mandatory retirement policies. A fortunate few have generous pensions that begin paying out at a certain age, making the decision to retire quite easy for them. Sadly, some people stop working because of serious health problems. This book is not about those individuals though their stories have lessons, too. They may face the post-retirement issues outlined above, but the decision to retire is relatively clear-cut for them.

Instead, this book is about the experiences of those who literally *chose* to retire from their long-term occupation. In the face of profound uncertainty, with so many big questions about what comes next (and "next" could potentially last a long time), how do people make such a consequential decision?

I decided that the best way to learn about the decision making process would be to speak with people who had recently retired or who were in the midst of retiring. I conducted semi-structured interviews from 2014 – 2017 with individuals who were gracious enough to share their experiences. I am truly grateful to them for their time and their candor. Their names and identifying details have been modified throughout this book to ensure anonymity.

Some readers may wish to explore every chapter in depth, gaining perspective from each of the interviews. Others might want to scan through the chapters to find respondents' stories that resonate more deeply for them.

Although each person's situation was unique, in most cases it seemed that a convergence of *internal* psychological factors and *external* circumstances propelled their retirement decision forward.

These stories are presented with my hope that it will help others who are grappling with the question of when to retire. To paraphrase one interviewee, "it's not easy to decide when to be done."

Chapter 2
Raymond's Story

Ray led a rich and varied professional life. His first job after college was in labor relations for an equipment manufacturer in Des Moines. He subsequently moved to Richmond, VA where he held multiple high-level human resource positions. A former boss then recruited him for a job in Detroit overseeing HR and labor relations at multiple locations for a large industrial firm.

Ray wanted to work for himself. He joined forces with his cousin to develop resort property near Vail, CO. The Savings & Loan crisis made it impossible for them to secure funding and thus their plans were derailed. Ray sold real estate for five years until his former boss solicited him yet again to join a growing manufacturing company, handling labor negotiations. In this role Ray oversaw the HR function in dozens of locations in the U.S. and Europe. Unfortunately the company's growth was unsustainable, and Ray (then in his mid-50's) was laid off along with over 200 colleagues.

Ever resilient, Ray soon found a job as Director of HR for a major manufacturer in Milwaukee where he stayed for 12 years. Ray retired in 2015 at age 68. He continues to do consulting and volunteer work.

When you were in the middle of your career, how did you view retirement?

I was raised in a very poor family. My parents were highly educated people but they never learned how to make money or put it away. I recall watching my mother cry because she couldn't pay the electric bill. When I thought about future retirement, my concern was about the type of life I would lead. I wanted to make sure that I didn't become impoverished. Throughout my life I've been very diligent (perhaps too much so at times) about watching my money and saving for retirement.

In what ways did your thoughts about retirement evolve and change over time?

When I got laid off I was leading an active, comfortable life. It was a real shock. My immediate boss, who was also let go, went into business for herself and it got me thinking about retirement in a more concrete way. I saw retired people who were bored or in poor health dying early. I wanted to avoid that. I started to give thought to how I might occupy my time. As much as I like golf I knew that I couldn't play it 5 days per week. But the reality is that I've never been a good planner; I'm a good "react-er".

At what point did you make a definitive decision that set retirement in motion?

In 2012 I was diagnosed with cancer and had surgery. It was a real eye-opener. My last boss and I had differences that made work feel quite stressful. I'm someone who likes to receive positive feedback and that wasn't my boss's style. And the cancer drugs were very hard on me. In 2014 my boss voiced concerns about my performance, so I decided it was time to pull the pin. I agreed with my boss that my performance had changed, and we agreed on a date for me to leave the firm.

How did you think/hope you would spend your time?

I figured that I could do some HR consulting and maybe some volunteer work.

So what was it like at first?

It was kind of weird for the first 6 months or so. I didn't have much direction. All my life I worked 50-70 hour weeks and I didn't have a lot of other interests. Then a friend asked me to help with some personnel challenges. That turned into an enjoyable four-month project. Other projects soon followed.

How does retirement feel compared to your work?

I've always enjoyed interacting with people even if the interactions were challenging. I've always liked to be needed. And I get satisfaction out of results. Those things are very much part of the volunteer work I do now with immigrants.

What advice would you give to others who are on the verge of making the decision – but haven't yet done so?

Make sure to work with a financial planner. I've seen people make the decision to retire only to have to return to work because they didn't have enough money. Also, spend some time really thinking about what you would like to do.

What has been different than you anticipated?

I've gradually accepted that I don't have to be number one at everything I'm doing. I'm able to be more relaxed about my performance; I didn't expect such a shift.

Anything else about the decision to retire that you would like to share?

If you're married your spouse is integral to the decision. My wife still works and it can feel awkward for her to go into the office while I'm out enjoying a round of golf. We've been able to talk it through though.

Observations about Ray's Retirement Decision

Ray strikes me as a remarkably resilient gentleman who does seem to have a knack for reacting adaptively to the twists and turns in his life. Though self-effacing, he displays a firm sense of self-respect and self-assuredness. The fact that he saved diligently for retirement no doubt made it easier for him to "pull the pin" (to use his term), but I wonder if his past resilience may have also played a role. Consciously or not, Ray probably felt reasonably confident that he would manage this next phase of life just as he had done so many times previously.

Chapter 3
Walter's Story

Walter is a 64-year-old gentleman who performs 8 to 10 hours of consulting work per week and plays golf daily. He struck me as one of the most contented individuals I had ever met.

Please tell me about your work

I come from an era in which our depression era parents taught us to work hard. Through hard work and if you were blessed with a modicum of intellect and ability, things would work out. I started working during the summers as a brakeman on the railroad. After taking a series of tests they recruited me into management. I stayed for 10 years, eventually becoming general manager of a division.

At age 32 I decided I didn't want to report to the same building for the rest of my life. I had attained the highest position I could there, and I didn't want to catch the 5:08 in the morning and the 6:15 at night for the rest of my career.

A former colleague convinced me to work for him as a regional manager at a privately held retail company. It wasn't intellectually stimulating but I was promoted to VP of operations and I stayed there for 6 years.

I saw an ad for President of a consumer products firm. I got the job, which paid three times what I had been making. I got a lot accomplished but I resigned three times because the owner of the company was a drug abuser who treated people very badly. I naively thought I could change him. He eventually died of a drug overdose.

I was then hired as President and CEO of a retail chain based in Houston. A few years later a larger firm acquired us and my new boss asked me to turn around their division in Chicago. I kept saying "no" because I loved what I was doing and I enjoyed my life in Texas.

At what point did you make a definitive decision that set retirement in motion?

I negotiated a good deal with my boss, moved to Chicago, and ran the division for 14 years. My boss eventually retired and I disliked working for his successor. In the meantime the company was starting to outsource functions within the business, compromising my role and my decision-making authority. The fact is when I run a business I put my heart and soul into it, but I need to have autonomy. I always said to my wife, "when I stop enjoying this I'll leave . . . I've worked hard all my life and I love working, but when it's not fun I'm out of there." And it wasn't fun for a solid two years. My new boss wasn't interested in my perspective or my ideas. So I began talking with my financial planner. I had reached the point where I was fully vested in the stock program, so I resigned and negotiated a payout package.

Is there anything that you were apprehensive, wary, or concerned about?

I was concerned that my outside interests just wouldn't be enough to keep me challenged intellectually and emotionally, and that I wouldn't get the same satisfaction in those roles that I got from the jobs I had.

So what was it like at first?

The first year there were so many loose ends to tie up that took a lot of time. I was happy playing golf and I served on 3 not-for-profit boards. I enjoyed those things, but they were not enough. So I began mentoring homeless families; it's a multi-year commitment and I meet with them weekly.

A friend said, "Walter, you'd really be outstanding at counseling and coaching executives." He urged me to get involved with an outplacement firm. I didn't want to work, but once I started dealing with executives it gave me the intellectual stimulation I wanted and I found it extremely rewarding. I found that people going through outplacement for the first time are like deer in the headlights. They really need guidance and help, and they need to understand their value and worth. I've always been a direct person and I coach them about possible next steps.

What advice would you give to others who are on the verge of making the decision – but haven't yet done so?

People who reach a certain age and level of success in their career should clearly understand who they are and what really drives them. They need to know what they enjoy about work so that they can find substitutes for it. They have to find interests, hobbies, or other things that give them the same level of fulfillment and satisfaction that their work provides. The need for fulfillment doesn't go away! The drive is still there for that. That's why I do the consulting work. I need recognition and rewards; that's important to me.

When I was at work I loved complexity and having issues to solve. When I showed up each day there would be several people waiting for me with problems that needed to be addressed. They were almost panic stricken. I loved bringing calmness and a thought process to it that helped them think in a logical, sequential manner. The consulting work satisfies that, and I do it 8-10 hours per week.

I'll discontinue the consulting when it stops being fun. If it feels like I'm not contributing to somebody or if the time commitment interferes with my quality of life, then I'll walk away from it. There's not a lot of longevity on my side of the family. I probably have 15 years left and so I'm going to do things that are rewarding. I've always had an incredibly positive attitude about life. Nothing bothers me (except my golf game)!

I'm thankful for my life. I love my children and they've done a good job raising their children. I managed to draw strengths from my parents about integrity and hard work, and I've always appreciated the blessings I've had.

Observations about Walter's Retirement Decision

Walter was keenly self-aware of his strengths and his interests, and he took advantage of them to seek out new challenges throughout the course of his career. Yet he also recognized when situations were unfixable (or as he might put it, "no longer fun") at which point he moved on. So how do we understand Walter's decision to retire rather than look for another senior executive position?

Walter had recently become vested in the company stock program, a noteworthy consideration. But my guess is that he also experienced some internal shifts. He cited an awareness that longevity didn't run in his family. And his new boss didn't seem to value Walter's strengths or interests. Perhaps he sensed that within the corporate sphere, his capacity to work hard and solve problems might no longer be seen as an asset. At a broader level, I wonder if he no longer felt the same sense of control over his professional destiny. To his credit, by retiring from a traditional executive role he created new opportunities to make use of his significant capabilities.

Chapter 4
Ben's Story

Ben is a 70-year-old gentleman who made a big career change in his early 30's. This led to a rewarding professional life that, upon reflection, prepared him well for retirement.

Please tell me about your work

For the first part of my career I was a social worker and my wife was affiliated with an education company. She was an independent contractor, working on commission and expanding offices in the West. The company felt that her territory had gotten too big and they wanted her to split her commission with another person.

We proposed that I would be her partner, and I ended up working for them for 37 years. If I had been doing the same thing all that time it would have been very boring and I would have left. Thankfully it kept changing.

At first we ran centers in Washington and then we were asked to move to California to take over operations there. We were there for 6 years at which point the company restructured and changed our status from independent contractors to employees. I was sent to London to open a center there while my wife ran a center in Los Angeles. It was not a fun time being apart. When I came back to the U.S. after 3 months I wanted to reside with my wife. My boss said, "you can have a job in New York City or be unemployed in Los Angeles". We had no ties in Los Angeles so we both transferred to NYC.

From my base in New York I was doing a lot of traveling, recruiting personnel and integrating the companies we acquired. Six months later our company approached us and asked us to move to Charlotte, North Carolina to work on a project. We kept our place in NYC and moved to Charlotte, although we came back to New York once per month to get our urban "fix". After doing this for 2 years our boss called and said, "we need someone in Chicago". We were happy to move to a big city, and I got involved in some high level projects at the state and national level.

When you were in the middle of your career, how did you view retirement?

I didn't have a conception of retirement early in my career. I was a social worker until the age of 32, and I never thought that I would ever accrue enough money to retire. Once we started working for the education company and had a decent income, we still had a lot of debt. It wasn't until the company restructured that our condition changed to the point that our only debt was the house. Starting then we were able to save and begin to think about retirement.

How did your thoughts about retirement evolve and change over time?

When we moved to North Carolina we figured that once our work was finished there we would ultimately retire back in New York City – not to just sit, but to enjoy the city. And we said the same thing when we moved to Chicago, but we like it here so we plan to stay.

What were the circumstances, concerns, etc. that led to your retirement decision?

I had originally planned to retire at 65, but my 401K was greatly diminished by the recession. I postponed retirement and stayed for 2 more years. In the end I wondered if I was being marginalized to some extent because I wasn't getting significant new assignments; those were given to younger colleagues. That said, the company was good to us from a salary and bonus perspective. I was concerned that there would not be enough work for me to continue doing this full time. There was no pension so I worked out a deal with them. For the last year (at age 67) they would pay my full salary and I would come in 4 days per week the 1st quarter, 3 days per week the 2nd quarter, and 2 days per week the remainder of the year.

It worked out well and there were no complaints. I could come and go as I pleased, I traveled, did board work, and I didn't have to be there daily. By the time I was going into the office 2 days per week I was already doing some volunteer activities, so it felt as if there was no adjustment at all to full retirement. Once I retired my company even called me back a few times to work on some things.

How did you think/hope you would spend your time?

I wanted to spend my time getting up and working out, but without feeling rushed. I wanted to do something constructive and I wanted to make sure I wouldn't get bored, so I volunteered. I was still traveling part-time for work so I opted for volunteer roles where I could control the commitment and control the hours. A former boss asked me to join him at a start-up, but I didn't want a full-time job. He said, "when you get bored call me". That was 2 ½ years ago and I haven't called him!

Did you have any misgivings or concerns about retiring?

My biggest fear was boredom. I think we moved 9 times in the 47 years we've been married. I don't believe we ever envisioned going someplace to retire (in a passive fashion) – other than the idea of settling in NYC. We didn't contemplate going to traditional retirement locations such as Arizona or Florida or Mexico. It never entered our thought process, and I never envisioned going somewhere where I'd just sit around doing very little. I never played golf. But I feared that I'd get bored and that we wouldn't have enough money to live comfortably.

How does your retirement seem compared to your work?

I miss the challenge of working with boards, but there is far less aggravation and frustration now compared to when I was working. I don't miss the long meetings and conference calls. Retirement means that I don't have to do any of those things I don't like doing.

I do miss contact with some of the people and I found that after a very short time I only had contact with two people from work. You spend your whole life with people day in and day out, do things socially with them, and then it just ends. I didn't think that it wouldn't end so abruptly but it did.

One of the issues when you move as much as we did is that it can be challenging to establish and maintain lifelong friendships. In California our friends were those who had children our kids' ages. We have a few close friendships with people who don't live here, and we've made some friend-ships in our building here in Chicago. These are people we enjoy being with, we spend time in each other's homes, but these aren't intimate friendships where we share close things. If there's a regret that would probably be it.

What advice would you give to others who are on the verge of making the decision – but haven't yet done so?

Aside from the obvious – figuring out your finances and making sure that you can do this – don't overthink it. Don't worry. I've talked to people who said they were concerned about having too much time on their hands, but now they're busier than ever doing things they want to do. I guess some folks worry about how they'll fill their time, or they fear that they and their spouse will get tired of each other. I haven't had that problem. I do think it's important that you find things for yourself if you're in a relationship, so that you don't have to be together all the time. When we travel we're together all the time, and when we get home I'm happy that I can be by myself for an hour or so. But I'd say that if you can manage it financially, do it!

What has been different than you anticipated?

I find that as I get older, my capacity for being un-scheduled is greater. I have breakfast and work out mid-morning. I come home, have lunch, take a short nap, and may or may not have something scheduled to do in the afternoon and that's ok. I don't feel a need to be scheduled. I volunteer at an agency for the blind, reading for visually impaired people one afternoon per week. I'm on the board of one organization and I do a little volunteer work for another. And I find that I'm not willing to schedule multiple things in one day. My days feel sufficiently full, and we're frequently out at night attending cultural events. Oh, and I still enjoy cooking.

Anything else about the decision to retire that you would like to share?

I was a psychiatric social worker in the Navy and then worked for multiple mental health agencies. When I got the opportunity to work with the education company, I told myself that if this doesn't work out I could always go back to being a counselor. But I earned so much more than I would have as a social worker and that gave me more options. One thing that helped with retirement is that my career required flexibility. I had to reinvent myself multiple times; I didn't think of it that way in the moment, but it does lend itself to adapting to retirement.

Observations about Ben's Retirement Decision

It would be easy to conclude that Ben's decision to retire was primarily based on finances. He continued to work beyond his intended retirement at 65 because his 401k had been battered by the recession. As important as financial security was for Ben, I believe that he needed something in addition. Ben spoke of how his flexibility served him well throughout his career and how it probably helped him adapt to retirement. My sense is that not only is flexibility one of Ben's strengths, it may also be one of his *needs*. Ben didn't want to be tied down to one role or one activity at work, and he was concerned that he might become bored in retirement. The thoughtful plan he negotiated in his final year of work provided him with a flexible schedule, and he had the time to explore volunteer activities. He was able to ease into retirement without feeling locked into a limited or restricted routine. Ben saw that he could come and go as he pleased without feeling rushed, bored, or unduly obligated.

Chapter 5
Sharon's Story

Sharon is a 64-year-old lawyer who has worked in a variety of settings. She began her career with a government agency and then she practiced in a series of law firms. She has been with her current firm for over a decade.

When you were in the middle of your career, how did you view retirement?

I'm part of a generation that said, "I don't want to work until I drop dead." Unrealistically many of us thought we would retire when we were 50, but when you get to that age it seems ridiculously young. So I didn't seriously think about retiring then, nor have I reached a point where I've hit our firm's mandatory retirement age. But I think I've always loved my work and my profession, so it's not been something I've wanted to escape from in any way. On the other hand I never thought I would work till the very last moment. I've got friends who say, "If I stop going to the office I'll die." I don't feel that way, so it's not as if I've been actively avoiding retirement.

How did your thoughts about retirement evolve and change over time? How would you characterize the shift in your thinking?

Well, as I said once I hit 50 it seemed too young. At the same time, I've wanted to make sure that I have an opportunity to enjoy some of the fun things I didn't have time to do because of work. I guess I got to the point that I was ready to make a change, and that's when I actively started to look forward to it. I see it as an exciting new challenge and a new chapter. I don't quite understand people who only want to work. I want to do other things.

At what point did you make a definitive decision that set retirement in motion?

Our law firm has some milestone dates that everyone has to attend to. I haven't hit any of the milestones yet, but knowing that they're out there does cause you to think about it a little more. At age 65, you serve at the pleasure of the executive committee on a year-to-year basis, and at 68 there is a hard stop date. The executive committee is charged with ensuring that people are still productive. You can opt-in early, which at age 64 is what I did. This begins a two-year step down period during which I will remain a partner. I can elect to do some work or no work. I can pick and choose what I want to do, including non-billable work involving committees and the community at large.

Is the flexibility here one of the things that helped you make the decision?

Yes. I realized that as I got closer and closer to the opt-in date, I hadn't told any of my clients that I was doing this. There was something in the back of my head that was making me hesitate telling them. I've had some clients for 20+ years and I have an emotional attachment to seeing their projects through. I hope that we'll be able to finish up in the next year. I don't know that I'll want to work through to the end of the two years because I believe that as time passes, the less attached I'll feel here and the more I'll have other interests out there. In the meantime it gives me something to do. I come in as needed. My client matters don't require daily involvement. I still have an office and a secretary, and I still have the support of the firm. It's not like a cold turkey separation.

As you reflect on your delay in telling your clients, what do you think was holding you back?

I guess I wasn't sure what was I going to do with myself on Day One when I began this two-year step-down period. It's hard for me to say to clients, "I'm going to be cutting back" if I don't know exactly what that means. I've worked almost every day since I graduated from law school and that's what I know how to do. I was also concerned about how it would feel to phone these people who've relied on me for many years. Sure, I could reassure them that it will be a 2-year transition and remind them that they know my other partners who have also worked on their matters, but frankly it seemed tantamount to saying, "I'm out of here. Thanks." I didn't want them to feel like I was dumping them.

Internally everyone here at the firm knew I was making the transition, but it's another matter to announce it to clients. For the most part when I did have the conversations everyone was great. The obstacle was really more in my head than it was a reality. And because of the two-year arrangement, I was able to say, "I'm going to be here. Your stuff will never fall through the cracks during the transition". Interestingly, this often started a conversation with some clients my age about *their own* retirement.

You opted to take the phased retirement. You had the choice of doing that or just stopping. How did you make that decision?

I think it was because I wasn't totally sure about what I was going to do with myself and so this gave me a little bit of a security blanket. I could say to myself, "I still have some things I'm working on, and that's something to grasp onto while I'm making this transition into whatever I decide to do next." Having the early opt-in gave me some structure, and there are others like me at the firm doing it. I didn't have to reinvent the wheel; it's been done for me.

My primary concerns were how will I occupy my time and what will feel most meaningful? And I have intentionally NOT committed to very many invitations. The good news is people start calling you and asking, "do you want to do this or that?" I haven't really made any commitments yet because I want to experience what it's like to have freedom and discern what I want to do with it.

One thing I know is that I don't want anything that is going to require me to be at a certain place at a certain time for a certain number of hours every day or even many days a week, because I've done that. If I wanted to keep doing that I would stay here and get paid for it.

That said I imagine I will find some volunteer activity that I will commit to at some point. I'm surveying the options right now. It's all about flexibility at this point because that's the one thing that you don't always have while working. You're accountable no matter what. I really want to be able to stretch and be more spontaneous.

How did you think/hope you would spend your time?

Hopefully I'll get to see my grandchild more often. And although I've lived here for decades there are vast parts of Chicago I don't know and so I'm in an exploration mode. It's easy and fun to visit new neighborhoods and see what's there.

A lot of people grapple with the rhetorical question, "what will you put on your business card after you retire?" If you're not an attorney, who are you?

I don't know. I didn't work for 2 years after my son was born. I felt a loss of identity very strongly back then because being a housewife wasn't integral to how I thought of myself. I had a new identity as a mom, but I missed my professional identity. I don't know if it will be as much of an issue for me now. I haven't been separated from work long enough to know for sure, but I don't feel it yet.

Do you perceive any difference in how you feel vis-à-vis your colleagues?

Yes, I felt a definite and sudden change in how I felt. I went from feeling like one of the key people here, to not being in the loop anymore. It feels a little funny when you've been a player in every-thing and now you're not, but you have to get over that. If you want to retire you don't get to have your cake and eat it too. People are super nice; it's just that they tend not to ask my opinion on things.

I tell myself I'm moving on, and if I want to do that then it makes sense that they will change, too. It's important that the younger people step up and start to take the reins.

In terms of your occupational status, what do you say to people?

I say, "I've just started a two-year phased retirement." Few people I speak with really understand exactly what that means. Granted, it's an unusual arrangement that my firm has but it provides me with the gradual exit ramp I wanted.

Did you have any misgivings or concerns about retiring?

My husband and I have done a good job on the financial side of things. We saved all along and managed to take care of the big life expenses such as our kids' education. My concern is, am I going to get to a point where having lunch with my girlfriends is not enough for me, and will I find something else I want to spend my time on? I'm not too worried about it because there are lots of opportunities out there in a city like this.

Are you and your husband at approximately the same point in retirement process?

Yes, he just went down to 80% and he plans to be fully retired in 2 years. We'll have to face some issues about how to spend our time and we don't necessarily see it from the same perspective, but hopefully after all these years we'll find a way to thread that needle.

What advice would you give to others who are on the verge of making the decision – but haven't yet done so?

In terms of the decision to retire, once you make that mental shift when the scale tips in favor of retiring, there is a corresponding internal question about whether to put forth the next bit of effort (e.g. to find the next client) or not. I noticed that when I fully embraced the idea that I was going to retire, I could tell that I was not extending the same level of energy compared to when I was totally committed to working. And the fact is, at that point you really do need to go ahead and retire because you're not doing your organization any favors.

I would also encourage people not to commit to anything initially. So many people I know have settled on one activity for their retirement, thinking it's going to be the right thing without really examining or exploring multiple possibilities.

Observations about Sharon's Retirement Decision

Knowing that the firm had a hard stop at age 68 made the prospect of retirement real for Sharon.

She was fortunate to be able to opt-in early to a phased retirement beginning at age 64. The two-year transition period provides her with an ideal combination of structure and flexibility, allowing her to let go of her responsibilities in a comfortable way. She can fulfill commitments to her clients while simultaneously exploring new possibilities and new routines. Most importantly it gives Sharon time to figure out what comes next. It is probably very comforting for her to know that she has two full years to start crafting a revised identity.

Chapter 6
Henry's Story

Henry is a 61-year-old gentleman with two married children. He was a general surgeon for 22 years in suburban Milwaukee. Prior to that he served and practiced medicine in the US Army for 10 years, including deployment during the first Persian Gulf War. His army training and experience was broad and varied, as was his surgical practice, ranging from reconstructive procedures to emergency room treatment of children.

When you were in the middle of your career, how did you view retirement?

I never really wanted to work forever. Although I loved my work my goal was to retire after 20 years. It pretty much turned out that way.

How did your thoughts about retirement evolve and change over time?

I was a surgeon, that's what I did. But it's not who I am. I knew that at some point I would have to stop but I also knew that I could enjoy myself in retirement and contribute to the world in other ways.

At what point did you make a definitive decision that set retirement in motion?

When I was 45 I developed chronic back pain. In subsequent years I tried to adapt by cutting back my hours and avoiding certain surgeries. I focused more on outpatient procedures. The pain medications I had to take weren't pleasant. In addition to that, the changes I saw coming in healthcare were not very appealing, including increased government regulation and diminished respect for the medical profession.

As my back pain got worse I thought that perhaps I could just focus on doing cosmetic procedures, but I knew that it wouldn't be as satisfying as the major surgeries I used to do. I considered trying to find an administrative role but I didn't think that would be rewarding. It got to the point where the pain was debilitating and disruptive. I just couldn't provide patient care any more. By that time I met the financial goal I had established. It wouldn't provide for a luxurious retirement but it would be enough.

What exactly was the decision?

I set a date to close my practice that coincided with the expiration of my office lease. It gave me time to meet commitments to my staff and patients.

How did you think/hope you would spend your time?

I wanted to be busy, spending time together with my wife of 35 years and pursuing hobbies. We wanted to move from suburban Milwaukee; it was a great place to raise a family but we didn't want to retire there. We were drawn to the urban lifestyle of Chicago.

Did you have any misgivings or concerns about retiring?

Not really. Being a surgeon is a terrific job but I didn't feel a profound sense of loss when I decided to stop working.

Back pain was a major factor in your decision to retire. You were robbed of your livelihood by a physical condition and yet you seem relatively at peace with it. How so?

As a surgeon I've seen many awful things and have met many people who struggled with terrible circumstances that were far worse than mine. In addition, my experience in the Persian Gulf War was truly horrific. The suffering around you is so bad that it makes you feel hopeless. Once you're home, when bad things happen you can put them into perspective and recognize that there's almost always a way out, a way to make things better.

So what was retirement like at first?

Pretty much as I expected. We were busy selling our home in suburban Milwaukee, renovating a condo in Chicago, and spending the winter at our place in Palm Desert.

How does your retirement seem compared to your work?

The "highs" from work were pretty great. I was able to help patients with complex surgical needs that no other surgeon would take on. That said, I find myself feeling just as satisfied now. I joke that when I was working I'd get up, shower, grab breakfast, read the paper, do the puzzles, and it would take me just 30 minutes. Now that I'm retired I do the exact same thing but it takes me 3 hours! Joking aside, I'm very busy. We're meeting new friends and enjoying cultural activities. I do a lot of cooking, yoga (which helps with my back), and I'm taking an improvisational acting class.

What has been different than you anticipated?

I feel so much better physically than I thought I would!

What advice would you give to others who are on the verge of making the decision – but haven't yet done so?

Don't worry about the details, but do give careful consideration to what will truly make you happy. Don't compromise on that. For us, living in a vibrant urban setting was important. We could have selected a larger residence elsewhere, but finding a great location where we could walk to everything was key to our sense of contentment.

Observations about Henry's Retirement Decision

One could easily conclude that Henry's decision was relatively uncomplicated. His back pain had become debilitating, and at that point his savings appeared sufficient to make ends meet in retirement. Perhaps it was really that simple, and yet I'm struck by how composed he was about being forced by pain to relinquish his career. My sense is that his experience in the Gulf war helped him accept and adapt to the reality of his circumstances. As he said, combat experience taught him that in the civilian world there is almost always a way to make things better. Having a hopeful, optimistic perspective about post-retirement life probably made it that much easier for him to make his decision.

Chapter 7
Arthur's Story

Arthur is a 75-year-old gentleman who retired four months prior to our interview. He served as CEO of a specialty metals firm for 34 years before handing over the reins to his youngest son.

Please tell me about your work.

I received my MBA and got snapped up by Xerox after graduation, but I didn't like the corporate culture so I decided to quit and join my father's tiny scrap metal firm. He had 5 employees. I spent 17 years there in what was a typical family business. But my father never incorporated it nor did he run it as a business. I had 3 siblings but I was the only one involved in the business. Dad didn't understand the fact that when *he* died the *business* would die. So I'm thinking to myself, if there's anything left to inherit I'm going to get 25% of it and then I have to give 75% of what I subsequently earn to my siblings. That wasn't fair and I explained that to my father. I said, "Dad, I've got four young kids that I have to support. We need a different arrangement." He said, "that's the way it is" and so I said, "ok, I quit." The day after I left we became best friends. He just couldn't have another bull elephant in his backyard. This story is relevant to my retirement, as you'll see shortly. We're all a product of our own history and experiences . . .

So I started this company. It's a completely different firm although in a similar industry. After a few years I came up with a real innovation that catapulted us from a startup to being a major player. The business did really well and we were doing just great. I raised four children and sent them all to college. Two of my kids ultimately joined me in the business, my eldest daughter and youngest son.

Then along came 2010, which was not a great year in my life. I was diagnosed with prostate cancer. My eldest daughter quit. And my two middle kids moved to California. That left just my youngest son and me. Here I'd had this whole life plan where I was going to make this business into a big conglomerate and have my four kids join me, and everything just dissolved. And by that point the 2008 recession had decimated our industry. Our business plummeted and we had to lay off roughly half of our workforce.

You really don't want to get cancer. I'm fine now, but I lost a whole year of my life. In 2010 we were in a free fall situation and I wasn't strong enough to run the business, so my son became President. He started running things and doing a very good job. But being the crusty old founder, it was hard for me to let go. The truth is I held on for 3 to 4 years too long. I shouldn't have done that. The equal truth is that I was foundering. I was behind the times in my intimate knowledge of the industry.

Many of our customers went out of business during the recession. We got to the point in 2015 where my son and I agreed that we had to close our doors. Instead we ended up with an unexpected opportunity to buy a competitor! We got a great deal and combined the two companies together. In less than a year the new entity was doing very well.

I still wasn't sure about retiring or anything else. As we were looking at the acquisition, it became obvious to me that I didn't have physical and mental stamina to run something this large. My son wanted to form a partnership with me. I started thinking about my own history and I realized that it needed to be structured so that he could be appropriately and fairly rewarded (while still allowing me to leave a small percentage of the business to each of my other three kids). We were really under the gun to figure out both our partnership agreement and the acquisition agreement by April 1st, 2016.

I had really not thought through the concept of retirement. And here it is four months later, and I still have a hard time saying, "I'm retired." It's really hard. And to be perfectly candid I wasn't ready for it either. I didn't have a life plan and a purpose, or a schedule of things to do every morning. I got up on April 2nd feeling empty.

The initial plan was that I would remain here as chairman, and I assumed that in that capacity I would be an advisor to my son. Well you know what I found out? My son really didn't want me to serve as an advisor. Now, I've since found out that it's not because he doesn't love me or doesn't think I'm smart. It's psychological. It's his turn in the sun. He's the CEO now. If I'm walking around here, people are listening to me too much. Even though they know he's the President and CEO. I felt so foolish, having gone through what I did with my father and unintentionally creating a situation where my son felt resentful. I'm such a dummy. I suppose that I sensed it but I didn't really realize it or act on it. There he was, feeling the way I did 40 years ago with my father. It's funny how that happened. So I've bent over backwards to make sure that I fixed it. And now he's running this entire show and he's doing a terrific job.

So the definitive decision to retire came during the acquisition period?

You know something Larry, if we hadn't gone through the acquisition I might still not have retired. But as I remember it my son said, "if you want to do the acquisition that's fine but either I'm running it or I'm out." He was absolutely right. I suppose that while I like to think of myself as a decent business manager I really wasn't a great personal life manager. I just acted without a real plan, without thinking about it. I just figured that if the company did well enough everything would take care of itself eventually.

When you were in the middle of your career, how did you view retirement?

That's a good question, but I never really thought about retirement. I was so busy doing what I was doing. One of the reasons why the business isn't even larger is that I coached every one of my kids' sports teams. I wasn't about to let making a living preclude my living. And thus I was busy with everything else in addition to the business. If the concept of retirement ever arose in conversation I'd say, "maybe some day I'll think about it." Hence my situation today.

So other than staying on as chairman what else did you imagine you would do with your time?

I enjoy golf and travel. So I suppose in the back of my mind I figured I'd become a snowbird and play golf all winter. Maybe take a few more trips. Beyond that I really hadn't thought about it. I'm looking at second career options. I'm taking un-dergraduate and graduate courses at a nearby university. But it's not enough. I never had a life plan that included retirement. To be candid, I'm still kind of lost. I don't have anything that's giving me a sense of purpose. I have some ideas about things that I want to do, but so far none of them has ignited to the point where I'm jumping in with both feet.

What advice would you give to others who are on the verge of making the decision – but haven't yet done so?

Clearly making a plan is really important and it's one of the things that I had never thought of. And consider your spouse. Never having thought about what I would do in retirement meant that I never thought about what *she* would do in retirement. She doesn't have a traditional job but she does a lot of volunteer work and she doesn't want to stop. So one piece of advice is to establish and maintain an ongoing dialogue with your wife. It sounds obvious but it never occurred to me.

The other thing is, you really must have some sense of what you might like to do. I don't have the patience to sit and do all the reading I thought I'd want to do. My biggest dilemma is that I'm not responsible for anything anymore. The buck always stopped right here (pounds desk) and now there are no more bucks! I'm comfortable financially but I don't have any more responsibilities. There's no place I have to be, no commitments I have to fulfill. And that's a real void especially when you've been the go-to guy for 35 years. This concept of not having responsibility is something I never anticipated. On the one hand it's a relief and on the other hand it's a huge void. And I look back on the last few months. What have I accomplished? I played a lot of golf. That's about all I did.

Just out of curiosity, what was your father's retirement experience?

My father never retired. He couldn't afford to do so financially. He died while he was still running his business. He died on a Sunday and on Monday I had to open his business and tell everybody that we were shutting down. That was not a fun week.

Observations about Arthur's retirement decision

Arthur's experience likely resonates for many readers. Most of us have known people who never seriously considered retiring, and they were caught off guard when circumstances forced their hand.

As Arthur spoke, it was clear that he was troubled by his situation. When the interview came to a close, he reiterated how uncertain he was regarding his ability to find a meaningful and compelling path forward. "I just don't like the *idea* of retiring" he exclaimed. "I know there are opportunities, but what I'm really afraid of is that nothing will grab me and that maybe I'm over the hill."

I pointed out to him that he was very much still in a period of transition and that given his history of resolving challenges, there was no reason to believe that he wouldn't emerge comfortably from this one as well. I noted that in his favor is the fact he is interested in a variety of activities and has the wherewithal to pursue them. I said, "Arthur, there are two things you should consider. It's more than just finding a compelling project; it's also got to have just the right amount of responsibility. That's going to take some time to find, a good deal longer than the four months that have passed since you officially retired. It's also important that you not become isolated. Stay out there talking with people about your ideas for what to do next. Don't forget, you didn't have a paternal model of retirement and so it may help you to get input from others."

I continued, "I understand your fear of not finding something meaningful to do, but I think that the bigger issue is that there are so many choices. In order to make a good decision you need information. For each of your many options you've got to drill down to determine whether it's suitable for you, and that takes some time and effort."

Arthur's decision to retire was far from planned, but it was a decision nonetheless. He could have refused to step down. Instead, he went through a period marked by acquiescence and emerging insight. He conceded to his son's insistence that he, not Arthur, run the show. Arthur became resigned to the fact that his health and stamina were not ideal for leading the company. Significantly, he eventually realized that he risked repeating his own history. In Arthur's story we see how external circumstances and internal, psychological factors converged in a way that brought about the decision to retire.

Chapter 8
Leslie's Story

Leslie is a 59-year-old Chief Financial Officer for an electronics manufacturer. I'm particularly grateful to her for making time to speak with me just one week prior to her last day at work in June, 2016.

Please tell me about your work

I started working in 1980 after graduating from the University of Michigan. I had a liberal arts degree in economics and went to work as an analyst for the Federal Reserve Bank. It was a pretty good first job. I worked there 2½ years. I also enrolled in the University of Chicago's MBA program part time in the evening. My husband was working and that allowed me to quit my job at the bank and pursue my studies full time. I received my MBA in finance and accounting, and sat for the CPA exam. With my degree in hand I went to work for a Big 8 accounting firm. After 2½ years there I joined the family business in 1985.

My father founded the firm and he convinced his brother to join him in the 1970's. We manufacture specialty electronics for the automotive industry. I started in a sales role because our sales person was out on maternity leave. It was a good way to get to know the business. When she came back I migrated into the finance and accounting position. My father sold the company to his brother in 1987 and exited over a 5-year period. I had an opportunity to buy some equity in the company and became a minority owner.

My uncle's son Chris came to work with us in 1990, and my uncle retired in 1994. Chris and I have been the de facto leaders of the business since then and it has grown substantially. As CFO I've been responsible for accounting, finance, information systems, and human resources. Our company has multiple plants, including locations in Mexico and China.

When you were in the middle of your career, how did you view retirement?

The business was always taxing and our clients were very demanding. My conception of retirement was getting to a place at which one could afford to do the things one wanted to. I often dreamed of having a business without customers. Throughout my tenure our business was continually changing to meet the needs of our clients. They wanted us to be nearby, which necessitated opening a location in Mexico. When I was in my 30's I was having my children. Those years were extremely busy and not a lot of fun. The obligations were significant and I had very little freedom with regard to many aspects of my life. When I turned 40, I felt a certain easing from the demands of motherhood and working full time.

How did your thoughts about retirement evolve and change over time? It sounds like it started as an abstract sense of freedom based on fewer obligations, but did it evolve into something more concrete?

The shift really happened when we sold the company. We began discussing succession starting way back in 2004. From 2004 until the sales transaction took place in 2012, we were working on growing the company and preparing it for sale.

It sounds like the concept of retirement was percolating in tandem with the succession decision.

Yes. I guess that brings up the deep feelings I have about the company itself and what we've built. My father founded the company, ran it with his brother, and my cousin and I expanded it to employ more people here and abroad. But as much as I'm proud of what we've accomplished, there are conflicting emotions. This is tiring, hard work. It's 24/7 and it's demanding. So while I'm keenly aware of the legacy we've established, at the same time I've felt a building sense of weariness. There has been a repetition of the same problems, the same people issues, the same barriers. That, for me, is the most compelling of my reasons for wanting to leave. I figure that I am still young enough and healthy enough to go out and find something different and interesting.

At what point did you make a definitive decision that set retirement in motion?

In 2011 my cousin Chris set a date of 2015 for his retirement. I thought that setting a deadline was an interesting approach. After the sale of the company closed in 2012, our board began working on the succession plan for senior management. Within those discussions I felt it was the right time and place to set a date for my retirement. So in the fall of 2013 I said it was time for the CFO position to change, and that I would step down in June 2016. My assistant Michelle had been here 14 years and so she was a logical successor. One of my reasons for wanting to move on was to give her an opportunity to move up. She's responsible for many of the improvements we've made here. That was a contributing factor in my decision to retire. I also felt that by taking this step it would set an example for others on the leadership team.

Did you have any misgivings or concerns about retiring?

I wonder about the new reporting relationships among our team that will emerge once I exit. People will need to adjust to different work styles, but I'm sure they will with time.

When I told the board in 2013 that I planned to retire I had some trepidation. There were some nights even in 2015 when I would wake up in a panic about it. I've been coming here for 31 years and this is going to be a big change for me. Even now when I try to comprehend intellectually what the change means, I really can't do it. I think about it every day. Will I be able to set goals and organize my life around them? Will I have the same meaningful, substantive exchanges with people and feel like I'm part of a group?

During the time since you made the decision, how did your feelings about retirement shift?

It's been a long time since I made the decision in 2013, but there were multiple matters that needed to be attended to before I could leave. The company was continuing to grow and there were many aspects of the transition that needed to be addressed.

But I'm not waking up in a panic anymore. You set a date to step down, and then it becomes something that's out there in the future that you're working towards. The trepidation I felt actually increased though 2015, but then as I got closer to my retirement date in June 2016 I became more certain that this really is the right thing for me and for the company. I believe that when you've had someone who has been in a position as long as I have, it's a real disadvantage to a company. I don't bring fresh ideas and fresh energy to problems, or new ways of doing things. I think that for senior management there ought to be something akin to term limits.

With regard to my sense of weariness, I was very influenced by my dealings with our Mexican subsidiary and the amount of time and energy it required. I had to travel frequently to work with the team there. It was a frustrating work environment and the hardest part of my job. So by the close of 2015 I was very tired of it.

How did you think/hope you would spend your time?

I foresee an initial phase of recharging. I'm not sure how long, perhaps three months or so. And then it's a blank slate for me. Conceptually what I'm looking for is to participate in some organization or entity that is learning-based, where I'm exposed to new things, where I can make a contribution without incurring excessive demands or obligations. My personality is action oriented. My husband is concerned that I'll be lost without a project. He's 4 years older and plans to work for about 3 more years before retiring. We'll have that difference between us to deal with.

I have this dream of going back to school. How common is that? I wonder about getting a Ph.D. in economics. I ask myself, "What would it take? Could I learn the math? Could I do the research? Am I kidding myself?" Though I don't have any firm answers, I know that I find myself most happy when I'm in a learning environment discovering new things and being challenged. How will I go about it? I'll be a little lost at first. I've been told about groups for people who are newly retired; it might be helpful to try that.

What advice would you give to others who are on the verge of making the decision – but haven't yet done so?

I can't think of any advice yet. Ask me in two months! Everything was put in place to ensure a smooth transition out of my role. But once I start being at home, that will be the challenge. I'm not close to anybody who has gone through retirement. As I say that out loud I guess it's the first time I've recognized it. My husband hasn't retired. My sister and brother haven't. My parents and in-laws' circumstances were very different. I feel alone in this in many ways.

Observations about Leslie's retirement decision

When Leslie made her decision in 2013 it made perfect intellectual sense. The business succession discussions, starting in 2004, provided a context for thinking about what the future might hold. Her cousin Chris clearly set an example in 2011 by announcing his own retirement date. The actual sale of the business in 2012 cemented the reality that eventually her role would be transferred to someone else. In addition, Leslie had a skilled long-term assistant who was well prepared to succeed her.

There were emotional factors at play as well, both contributing to her decision and resulting from it. She had grown weary from the repetitive demands of the business. The frequent trips to Mexico had become draining. And Leslie had become convinced that new ideas and new leadership would help her firm in the future. Her concerns about retirement are understandable. She hasn't yet established meaningful goals that will serve to organize her time and keep her engaged with others. The process feels like uncharted territory for her as it does for many. Retirement can offer great freedom, but with that can come uncertainty. I'm inclined to think that Leslie will fare quite well. Although she is grappling with the unknown she is inquisitive, action-oriented, and she lives in a large metropolitan area that provides her with ample opportunities and endeavors to choose from.

Chapter 9
Brian's Story

Brian is a 53-year-old gentleman who worked 30 years for a petrochemical firm. He started as a technician and then rose through the organization. When he retired, his title was director of quality assurance and compliance.

When you were in the middle of your career, how did you view retirement?

It was something I was always conscious of. I started at the company during my first year of college. I began thinking about my retirement because my uncle also worked there, and he had given me great advice over the years about how to plan for retirement. When I started there the company was growing incredibly fast and the stock price was rising to the point that it looked like I might even be able to retire at 40! The rapid growth didn't continue, but throughout my tenure retirement was something I was planning for (although I didn't have any specifics about how I would manage the transition or what I would do post retirement). I looked at it as very much a financial matter.

How did your thoughts about retirement evolve and change over time? How would you characterize the shift in your thinking?

I definitely started thinking about it more as I got older. I knew that at age 50 I would be eligible to receive a partial pension and the amount would increase each year thereafter. Shortly after turning 50 I attended a company seminar that explained the retirement program in greater detail. Something about it felt more real then.

At what point did you make a definitive decision that set retirement in motion?

After attending the seminar, I figured I would retire at 55 because that is when there would be a substantial increase in the pension amount. And then things changed! My boss, Alison, got a new boss and the environment shifted dramatically.

Alison's new boss didn't like her or anyone who reported to her, including me. The company changed too; a European conglomerate acquired us. We were told that we would be a different company, but nobody had a clear sense of what that would entail. It soon became apparent that we would operate with different values and different expectations. Alison left after a year. A few months later her replacement Diane arrived and we hit it off. This was roughly two years ago.

Diane asked me to take on a different role, but I was reluctant to accept it. I didn't feel comfortable with the new assignment although I sensed that I had little choice. I was being asked to do things I wasn't well versed in and mistakes were being made that I was responsible for. It was very uncomfortable. I wanted to leave at that point even though it was earlier than I'd planned. I also didn't care for the new company leadership and their approach.

I discussed it with my partner who was concerned about how retiring earlier than planned would impact us as a couple. He thought that perhaps I ought to give it a chance. And I felt that I should lead by example. If management asked me to take on something new I ought to do so. So I gave it a try for a year but it was incredibly stressful. It became a countdown; could I make it to 55?

After that year I sat down with a financial analyst. Thankfully it turned out that I could retire right then at age 52 if I wanted to. But my partner still wasn't fully on board yet. So I stuck it out for one more year. My stress level increased to the point that I went back for a few visits with a therapist I'd seen years earlier. We talked about whether or not I should stop working. Perhaps at some level I was looking for permission to retire, and the sessions helped me examine what it actually meant to be "done" working. I hadn't planned much for what would come next although I was comfortable allowing things to unfold.

What exactly was the decision? (e.g. setting a date, settling on a location)

Given my feelings about upper management, I was concerned about how the firm would respond to me once I announced I was retiring. I looked at the timing of when bonuses and stock grants would be issued and I waited until after that point to inform the company. My final day was roughly two months later.

When you made the decision, how did it feel?

Once I made the decision I still felt anxious that something bad would happen at work. But I worried a lot less than before. I also started using some of my vacation time and that provided a sense of relief. The number of emails I received started to taper off. Perhaps people realized that eventually I wouldn't be coming back, so maybe they started to solve matters on their own or they asked someone else.

How did you think/hope you would spend your time?

I thought I would spend my time exactly as I'm doing right now. I do a lot of maintenance projects around the house that I didn't have much time to work on before. I have more time to work on the garden and to entertain. I haven't started traveling yet but I will be doing more of that shortly.

Did you have any misgivings or concerns about retiring?

None at all. I have not regretted a single minute, felt badly, or thought about work. When my father retired he said that his only regret was that he hadn't done it sooner, and that always stuck in my head. I know that I'm incredibly fortunate. I got good advice, I planned well, and I was successful in my career. I can't imagine how hard it is for those who don't have enough savings to retire and are stuck in a stressful or unpleasant job.

So what was it like at first?

Every day feels like a weekend! My routine is very much like what my weekends used to be. There's no alarm in the morning but I still get up early, although not at 4:30 a.m. like I had to do when I was working. Now I get up around 6:00 a.m. I noticed after 2 weeks that my sleep had improved. Before I retired I couldn't remember the last time I slept through the night. Now more often than not I sleep soundly all the way through. I work on projects around the house that I used to feel pressured to fit in on the weekend.

I'm comfortable allowing a routine to emerge, and I'm not concerned about becoming bored. My partner is somewhat different. As someone who prefers more structure, he's curious and a bit incredulous about how easily I've adjusted to not having to go to work. I don't give it much thought but such a huge change in routine strikes him as rather unsettling.

How do you decide what to do each day?

For me it's very unstructured. I just look at the various projects I'd like to tackle and I work on them as time permits. I'm not worried about being bored, and if I do get bored that doesn't bother me. Something interesting will come up.

One thing that I gave a lot of thought to was "what did I want to accomplish in my career, and to what degree did I manage to do so?" Reflecting back, I realized that I had achieved what was most important to me. That insight was very comforting for me and it helped me make the decision to retire. I think that I had been worried that I might regret leaving too soon, but as I took stock of what I had done I felt more comfortable leaving.

How does your retirement seem compared to your work?

Over the years, work had become increasingly difficult including a grueling commute. I don't have that hassle any more. I truly liked the people that I worked with, but they weren't close personal friends so I don't miss the social aspect of work. For me, I didn't need to find suitable replacements for the satisfactions of work. I have lots of other interests to pursue. I love being outside and wish that I could make up for all the hours I had to spend inside at work.

What advice would you give to others who are on the verge of making the decision – but haven't yet done so?

I'd say take the time to think about whether you accomplished what you wanted to, or at least ask yourself are you satisfied with what you've accomplished? That process of self-reflection helped me be o.k. with the decision to leave. I'm aware that at 53 it's pretty early to be retired, and I was concerned that I might regret stopping at such a young age. Perhaps I wouldn't have been grappling with this if I was 65.

Has it been different than you anticipated?

Not really. It's not glamorous or anything. It's not like I'm going on a cruise around the world. But I also gave myself permission that I don't have to have it fully figured out. I worked for thirty years straight. The longest vacation I ever took was two weeks, and that was just recently. So I can take a year off and figure it out.

Observations about Brian's retirement decision

From a financial perspective, Brian put a good deal of thought into his retirement plan. Unfortunately, like so many people he had to contend with an unexpected change in circumstances at work. A new company culture, new leadership, and new job demands left him extremely uncomfortable. These changes also led him to begin contemplating retirement years earlier than he anticipated. Brian knew that he was financially able to retire, and he seemed confident that he would figure out how to occupy his time. But he needed to give himself permission to leave an increasingly unpleasant work situation, and he also needed to convince his partner that this huge shift in their domestic routine would turn out o.k. My sense is that he made excellent use of his counseling sessions; the self-reflection led him to conclude that he had accomplished something sufficient and meaningful at work. Armed with this sense of satisfaction, Brian could confidently transition into retirement even without a detailed plan for how to occupy his time.

Chapter 10
Beverly's Story

Beverly is a 64-year-old clinical psychologist. She formally retired roughly a decade ago, and she is now self-employed on a part time basis.

Please tell me about your work

After I received my master's degree I got a job as a counselor at a local mental health center. I truly enjoyed the work, my clients, and my colleagues. The role provided me with enormous intellectual and emotional satisfaction, so much so that I stayed there for several decades. The job also gave me the flexibility to be an active mom, and it provided my husband the security to launch his own business.

I've been a dedicated lifelong learner. I continued to take courses and eventually completed my Ph.D. A few years later, funding cuts impacted my job at the mental health center so I decided to retire from that position. Soon thereafter, once my children were launched, I decided to pursue my dream of opening a private practice.

Earlier in your career, how did you view retirement?

It seemed so far off that I really didn't think about it. That said, as I began to think about having a private practice some day, I viewed it as something I could possibly do once I retired from my job at the mental health center.

At what point did you make a definitive decision that set retirement in motion?

The funding cuts at the mental health center were quite dramatic. The job no longer offered the same satisfactions, and it seemed like the perfect time to pursue my dream of seeing clients on my own. I'm lucky that I was able to remain involved in my profession even though I formally retired from my job. This wasn't accidental. I tried to plan my career so that I would have options.

So what was it like at first?

I'm doing what I always wanted to do. I see several clients each week, and I have the freedom to travel and pursue educational interests. But I don't have the energy I once had. Physical injuries take longer to heal. If I decided to wind down my practice, I would still want to volunteer my skills as long as I can. I would also want to remain involved in continuing education classes. Intellectual and social stimulation is vitally important to me and I enjoy being around other scholar-practitioners.

What advice would you give to others who are on the verge of making the decision – but haven't yet done so?

When you're in your 40's and 50's be sure to start reflecting on your values. Think about what gives your life purpose, but keep in mind that you may not have the same energy when you're in your 60's. The process of discerning your values and finding outlets for them takes time. If you wait until the last minute (before retiring) to do it, it can be anxiety provoking if not downright paralyzing.

Observations about Beverly's Retirement Decision

Beverly was in a favorable position when the mental health center she worked at lost much of its funding. Her peers might have scrambled to find jobs at other agencies, but Beverly had a compelling desire to operate a private practice and she had already completed advanced training in psychology. The decision to stop working full-time in a clinic setting seemed to come relatively easily to her. Retiring gave her the freedom to pursue her dream, and she continued to derive meaning and satisfaction from helping others. This new arrangement also gave her the flexibility to adjust the number of clients she accepted based on her travel and educational schedule.

Chapter 11
Nathan's Story

Nathan is a 64-year-old gastrointestinal surgeon who retired 4 months prior to our meeting.

Please tell me about your work.

I went to medical school at Emory University in Atlanta. I returned to my hometown of Chicago for a residency at Lakeside VA hospital and eventually joined a busy practice in the suburbs run by an older colleague. He retired two years later and I stayed there for over 30 years, building it up to a six-physician practice with additional nurse practitioners. But with all of the regulatory and insurance changes, the practice became cumbersome and inefficient. I officially retired 4 months ago. My wife and I have three children. They're all grown and independent, and we sold the home where we raised the kids and moved to another suburb where the taxes are more reasonable.

When you were in the middle of your career, how did you view retirement?

I've had a longstanding opinion that it would be best to retire reasonably early. I had witnessed too many people who stayed on too long, thinking they could work forever. I saw this in medicine but I suspect it's true in other professions such as law and even teaching where people lose some of their effectiveness. I've always been conscious of the need to retire when you're still at the top of your game while you're still reasonably productive.

Back then I also had the foresight to save for retirement. Setting up pension plans from day one was very important. My intention and my hope was that once our kids were launched and independent we could sit back and enjoy life, assuming we had the health and means to do so.

How did your thoughts about retirement evolve and change over time? How would you characterize the shift in your thinking?

I stayed pretty true to my plan. That said, over time the industry evolved and I became a little less intensely driven about what I was doing. Even mid-career I would take on tough cases and I wanted to do it all. The further along I got though, I realized that I didn't need to do the 5-hour surgeries or take on the high-risk patients. Those things were no longer ego-fulfilling goals. At that point I started taking on junior partners and delegating some of the work. They had more current training and I realized where I was on the historical arc of medical progress.

Part of it too is that over time, given my family life and my multiple outside interests, I didn't feel as if my identity was just that of being a doctor. Often I look around and see other professionals who have nothing else other than their work.

At what point did you make a definitive decision that set retirement in motion?

That was about a year ago. Prior to that I just had this nebulous idea that I would retire some time between age 65 and 70. I really didn't have a target date in mind. About a year ago it really did dawn on me that maybe some of my surgical attributes are not what they should be. Maybe I didn't have the confidence in the operating room that I should have. No specific incident took place. I was simply trying to be alert and mindful about how I was feeling and performing, and I was seeing changes in other people who were older than me.

I realized too that my partners were performing a lot of the newer techniques and procedures, doing minimally invasive surgery with robots and so forth. I was less and less a part of that, although my partners appreciated my experience and deferred to me when patients needed challenging major operations. It was reassuring that I could add value. We got along very well and I felt gratified that I had put together a terrific team and that my legacy was established.

Tell me more about the circumstances, concerns, etc. that led to your decision.

As a doctor I had an appreciation of my own mortality. I've buried some good friends who were younger than me. A friend's widow encouraged me to "get out there and smell the roses." Knowing that I enjoy good health and have the means to enjoy other ventures was important. It helped knowing that I was out of debt and the kids were taken care of.

As I mentioned earlier, I also sensed that perhaps I was losing some of my confidence, if not my skills. The practice is well positioned to survive but the changing nature of medicine also introduced a lot of frustrations. All the regulations from the government and the insurers have really intruded on my ability to forge connections with my patients. Taking call in the middle of the night was becoming onerous as well. When you're younger you can get up in the middle of the night, run to the hospital to take care of someone, then come home and fall asleep and be fully functional the next day. When you're past 60 that's pretty tough!

How did you think/hope you would spend your time?

I hope to travel more. I enjoy playing golf and sailing. I like gardening and have been volunteering at a botanical garden working on trail maintenance and plant propagation. I get quite a bit of pressure from retired colleagues to maintain my clinical skills. They urge me to work with indigent patients abroad. I did it years ago but I'm not sure that it would be a good fit for me now. Perhaps some care is better than no care, but I feel that I've left the operating room (literally and figuratively) and to return on an episodic basis isn't a wise practice. I also want to spend more time with my grandchildren. For so much of my professional life I didn't have enough time for my children. I'd like to be more of presence in my grandkids' lives, taking them places and helping them explore their interests.

Did you have any misgivings or concerns about retiring?

I was concerned about the economics and my financial advisor did suggest working a little longer but I replied, "you aren't the one getting up in middle of the night and you're not the one dealing with self-doubt." As I looked at the numbers I concluded that we should be able to have a reasonable retirement. Nothing lavish, but I think there's enough to take care of my wife and I until the end. I do worry about the many people I see who don't save. They live extravagantly but they haven't put anything away.

The other question was, will I be able to keep myself busy? For the four months so far it's been o.k. It's been warm so I've been able to enjoy gardening, sailing, and golf. I'm not sure what it will be like when it gets really cold outside. You can only clean the basement so many times! I got involved in a lecture series at the University of Chicago, so I may do more of that in the winter. My wife's friends jokingly ask her whether I've driven her nuts yet or tried to alphabetize the spice rack. I've seen enough guys make that mistake so I'm careful. I try to be more helpful around the house. We've established a new rule that only one person is allowed in the kitchen at one time!

So what was it like at first?

I'm happy so far. It's been a relief not having to be at a certain place at a certain time. I still get up at 5:30 every morning. When you've done that for 40 years it's hard to change.

How does your retirement seem compared to your work?

Retirement has been intellectually satisfying and I've kept myself occupied, but I'm not burdened by the same sense of obligation and stress. When you see 15-20 patients in a day, you're shouldering their problems and you feel responsible for the outcome of their treatment. When you're first starting out you feel a sense of infallibility. Later in your career you realize all the things that can go wrong and so the stress is greater.

As you reflect back on your perspective about retirement and your decision making process, were you at all influenced by previous generations – what you saw a parent or grandparent go through?

To a certain extent. My father was a physician and I have two siblings who are also physicians. My older sister and my father both retired prematurely because of illness. My father retired at 64, earlier than he wanted to because he had become physically disabled. My sister was a partner in our practice and she retired due to a stroke. They both managed to have decent medical outcomes and went on to have happy post-professional career lives. They had multiple interests before retirement and they keep themselves occupied. Seeing them do well in retirement gave me the confidence that it would be o.k. for me too, that I could continue to have a meaningful life. People ask me what I did for a living and I reply, "I was a doctor." My wife corrects me and says, "you are a doctor." I don't focus on that as my identity. It's not the most salient aspect of who I am right now.

What advice would you give to others who are on the verge of making the decision – but haven't yet done so?

I think the one thing I'd say is that you need a certain element of structure. Mine isn't rigid, but it's enough to keep me busy. There's also a human need to feel that you've accomplished something. I always made it a point to thank my employees each day for a job well done. They left knowing that they made a difference. That's important for all of us, even in retirement. Find something that allows you to feel worthwhile and appreciated. Somebody else has to perceive value in what you're doing.

How did your retirement discussions with your wife go?

I confided in her first. I said that I'd reached my limit and I want to give my junior partners advance notice. She said it was my decision and she would endorse my choice. She was a little concerned about whether I would be content with my decision. Not a week goes by that I don't reassure her that I'm happy I retired when I did. We give each other enough room to do things. She's an avid golfer and she stays busy and committed. We're not attached at the hip. I like to travel more than she does. I like to sail; she doesn't care for it.

Observations about Nathan's retirement decision

Nathan had a long-standing desire to retire "reasonably early" while he was young enough to enjoy various pursuits and before his medical skills waned. As he neared retirement he was particularly vigilant about his performance. He noticed that his techniques were no longer cutting edge. He didn't have the same physical stamina and resilience he once had. He no longer felt the same drive to perform impressive surgical feats; to the contrary he was increasingly cognizant of what could go wrong and he started to feel less confident.

Nathan's father and sister served as positive role models for him. They found ways to enjoy a meaningful retirement despite their health challenges. Nathan had become increasingly frustrated by new rules and regulations impinging upon his practice. Seeing that his junior colleagues had become proficient and knowing that his legacy was established, it was easier for him to decide to step away.

Chapter 12
Charles' Story

Charles is a 65-year-old structural engineer who retired three years ago. After retiring, he and his wife moved from Indiana to Idaho.

Please tell me about your work.

For the last 27 years of my career I worked for a US Government agency located in northwest Indiana. The office was a great place to work, I had terrific colleagues, and we enjoyed raising our kids there.

When you were in the middle of your career, how did you view retirement?

I always hoped I would be able to retire while I was still physically able to do the things that I didn't have time to do while working. For some people, retirement is not part of the picture. Their whole identity is tied up in their work. I'm not that type of a person. For me personally, if people don't know that I used to be an engineer, that's fine. It's part of who I am, but there are other things I wanted to do.

My wife and I always wanted to live in the mountains of Colorado, but family kept us in Indiana. When I first joined the office I thought maybe I could spend most of my career there, and then transfer to a Western office for the last few years. I always knew that I would retire when I was young enough that I could still do things and not sit in a rocking chair. So early on, that was part of the mental equation for me.

How did your thoughts about retirement evolve and change over time? How would you characterize the shift in your thinking?

I had hoped I would be able to retire at 57, which is the minimum retirement age for my division. When that time came I was happy to let it pass for two reasons. Financially I wasn't really comfortable retiring at that stage, and then there was the psychological component. You've got to be psychologically ready, and at age 57 I was not ready to retire. Some people can do it, but I simply wasn't ready.

At what point did you make a definitive decision that set retirement in motion? What happened between age 57 and when you retired at age 62?

One of my concerns was, what would I do in retirement? How will I stay busy? This was one of my wife's concerns for me too. I can't just sit around. Don't get me wrong; I'm not trying to be critical of those who are happy to sit and read or whatever they wish to do. It's just that I'm not very good at it. Around age 58 I got together with a friend who I consider very Type A. He was extremely busy and happy in retirement. I thought, if *he* can enjoy retirement maybe I can too. It created a new psychological mindset for me. It was the first time I thought, "maybe I can be happy in retirement."

The encounter with your friend left you feeling more open and curious about retirement. Were there other things that led you to make the decision?

At my government agency there are common retirement points. The minimum age for retirement is 57. At 60 I became fully vested in my pension plan. And at age 62 there is a small boost to that pension. When I turned 60 I still wanted to keep working and wasn't quite ready to retire. My wife hadn't retired yet and she wasn't keen on me retiring before her. So as I neared age 62, I knew that would be the time for me. Also it was common for people in my department to retire at 62, and I didn't want to be the oldest one left. I stopped working a month after my 62nd birthday. My wife had retired several months before me. And by that point our kids were no longer living in Indiana.

How did you think/hope you would spend your time?

We had planned all along to move to the mountains of Colorado. We spent a lot of time there on our vacations and we loved it. However, we actually ended up in Idaho. Our daughter attended Idaho State University and married a young man from Pocatello. My wife suggested that we look around, so every time we went to visit our daughter we checked out different parts of the State.

We moved to a community about an hour away from our daughter, not knowing anyone there. We were really concerned about that. You start from ground zero meeting people. Think of how you typically meet people: through work, through your kids, or through church. Well we didn't have those things when we got here. Our first month here I was playing golf with someone and he mentioned that I should join the local Newcomers Club.

We rapidly started making great friends through the Club. Idaho gave us the hiking, biking, golf and skiing we were looking for in retirement, but to have this wonderful way of making new friends was a huge bonus for us. A common refrain you hear from people in the Club is "I have a busier, more active, and larger social life here than I ever did when I was working!"

Did you have any misgivings or concerns about retiring?

My single biggest concern was, could I keep myself busy doing fun, interesting things or would I be sitting home all day? My wife and I ask ourselves, if we were still in Indiana what would we be doing? I'd probably be playing golf (which I like) but I wouldn't want to do it everyday. I wondered would I find ways in retirement to be active in a fun way? The answer has been a resounding "Yes."

How does your retirement seem compared to your work?

I truly loved my job. It was fulfilling work and I loved it because of my colleagues. That said, I was ready to retire and I'm loving retirement more than I anticipated. It's better than I thought. I was psychologically ready, financially we were ready, and so far I'm healthy enough to enjoy it.

What advice would you give to others who are on the verge of making the decision – but haven't yet done so?

You need to make sure you have the financial resources. The websites that suggest you need a certain percentage of your pre-retirement income are probably underestimating how costly it is. I haven't found retirement to be cheaper than when I was working. Psychologically, you have to think about how you will be engaged with people and activities. My wife and I and lot of our friends do volunteer work. Think about how are you going to spend your time. You've got to have an idea about what you're going to be doing. You don't need to know the specifics, but you have to have a general sense of what would be satisfying. Our kids make fun of us because they have to schedule time with us. We're as busy as we've ever been.

What has been different than you anticipated?

I didn't anticipate how many friends I would develop. We joined a golf club when we got here and I made some friends there, but the Newcomers group has filled our broader needs for socializing.

Anything else about the decision to retire that you would like to share?

It wasn't an overnight or impulsive decision. It's something I thought about long and hard leading up to it.

When I retired one of the interesting things I heard people say was, "it took me months to unwind." I don't care if you're a UPS driver, a factory worker, or a farmer, there's a background level of stress that comes from working. It's part of your life. For me, the day after I retired it disappeared. It was a dramatically different feeling right from the start. It was a nice little bonus that I hadn't anticipated.

Observations about Charles' retirement decision:

Charles seems truly fortunate. He had a vision of a healthy, vibrant retirement and he took steps to make it a reality. The external circumstances that contributed to his retirement decision included the pension bump at age 62, the fact that most of his colleagues retired by that point, and the reality that his children had moved away – freeing him to relocate to the mountains he enjoyed so much. Internally, Charles was driven by a desire to retire while still young and physically active. His encounter with a friend who enjoyed retirement was also pivotal. It gave Charles hope and a new perspective about the possibility of remaining busy and engaged.

Chapter 13
Maureen's Story

Maureen is a 65-year-old physician who retired three years ago. She is married to Charles, profiled in the previous chapter.

Please tell me about your work.

I was an orthopedic physician for 30 years. I started as a solo practitioner and then 6 months later joined a multi-specialty group with two other orthopedists and twelve other physicians. We set up our own outpatient clinic. We were some of the only independent doctors in town, not linked with a larger hospital system. That helped because I was able to put money into our practice and take money out when I retired. Also, the cost of living in our city was quite reasonable, the schools were good, and so we didn't need to pay for private tuition for our kids. All those things added up to being able to afford to retire.

Earlier in your career, how did you view retirement?

I really didn't think about it much. I loved my career and I just sort of plodded along as I suspect most people do. My oldest partner practiced until he was 68. He still had great medical skills but he finally decided he wanted a lifestyle change. I was the second one to retire in my group. I hadn't really thought very much about retirement. I guess I just imagined there would be a time when it would make sense to retire, and eventually that time arrived.

Was there a shift in your thinking, or a point when you made a definitive decision to put things in motion?

I loved the partners in my group, I loved my patients, and I loved what I did. Unfortunately, computerized medical records created a problem. I'm not a typist; I got a "C" in typing. Although our first computerized record system was actually pretty good, we had to go to second system because of new federal requirements. The government mandated that we must assess and monitor various medical conditions. We had to document that we asked every patient certain questions (in order to prove that we were indeed monitoring those conditions). We would be penalized if we didn't ask these questions, but they were nonsensical. Whoever wrote the questions had no idea about healthcare. It just got to the point where I was spending more time doing paperwork than focusing on my patients, and that's not why I went into medicine.

Doing all the paperwork was adding up over the course of years, but the nail in the coffin was that second medical record system. It did one thing well and everything else badly! I would end up spending a huge amount of time at the end of my day typing in data, checking tests, etc. I got neck pain from all the hours at the computer. So I said to my husband, "it's getting to be *that* time." He said we could afford to do this, and so we decided to retire.

How did you actually put the decision into motion?

We had an agreement in our practice that when someone wanted to retire, they would provide at least 12 months advance notice. It takes a long time to recruit a physician to our city in Indiana. I let them know I wanted to retire, and they asked me to postpone leaving until June of the following year when medical residents graduate and it would be easier to hire someone. I agreed, but when June came they still hadn't found anybody so I worked on a per diem basis for another month. I didn't want to leave them in a lurch.

How did you think/hope you would spend your time?

I hoped to learn to cook because after 40 years of marriage I still don't know how! I'm enjoying taking cooking lessons now.

Did you have any misgivings or concerns about retiring?

We figured we would leave Indiana eventually, and neither of our children returned here after college. We like to ski and hike, so we knew we'd be moving somewhere else. The question was, where? But then our daughter moved to Idaho and it became an easy choice for us because of all the recreational opportunities there. Our concern was how would we meet people? That was a big deal because I developed friends through my work, through the kids' school, and through our neighbors. Fortunately we've met so many terrific folks through the Newcomers Club.

My dad is 95 and he lives in Columbus, OH. I was initially concerned about leaving the Midwest and being so far away from him. My sister lives nearby and is able to look in on him and I fly back there regularly, so I feel o.k. about that now.

So what was it like at first?

After I retired we stayed in town for about nine months because my husband was still working. We put our house on the market early thinking it would take a long time to sell, but it sold quickly. So we rented a townhouse. We had four weddings to attend so we decided rather than moving to Idaho and having to fly back we would just stay put temporarily. It was awfully boring. Most of my friends still worked. Once we moved to Idaho things changed completely. Now I have to search through my calendar to find time to do things.

How did you make the shift away from your professional identity?

I do know a lot of people who stay physicians their whole lives and want to be referred to as "doctor". When I was practicing I introduced myself to my patients as "doctor", but I did not refer to myself that way to any other people because I wasn't *their* doctor. After retiring I thought I would do volunteer work with the VA because anywhere I practiced I would need to have liability coverage. But they had no volunteer programs here whatsoever. I renewed my license twice in Idaho thinking that maybe something else would come up, but nothing did so I recently let it expire. I loved what I did, but I don't think my whole personality was wrapped up in it. I do know docs who are like that, but I've always had lots of outside interests.

What advice would you give to others who are on the verge of making the decision – but haven't yet done so?

I would say whatever you like to do, you should find a place where you're able to do it. Don't worry about leaving your comfort zone of where you've lived and worked. Where you lived while working might have been great for that phase of your life, but it might not be the best fit for when you retire. You should go to where you are able to do the things you love to do. People asked us, "how could you leave your home?" It's true that it was our home for over 30 years. It offered a place to build our careers and a place to raise our kids, but our kids weren't coming back and it was time to move on.

What has been different than you anticipated?

I'm WAY busier than I ever thought I would be. Yet I'm also able to enjoy things more. We used to rush through breakfast while getting ready for work, and now I can savor my coffee while listening to the birds and taking in the scenery here. Retirement is far better than advertised!

Observations about Maureen's retirement decision

Like her husband Charles, Maureen acknowledged that feeling financially comfortable helped her decide to retire. Of course feeling able to afford retirement is different than *being ready* to retire. In Maureen's case, both internal and external factors contributed to her decision to retire.

Internally, Maureen found it relatively straightforward to move beyond her identity as a physician. It was never the single defining element of who she was, and the fact that she was able to resign from her practice over time probably made the transition even easier. Maureen was initially concerned about moving so far away from her elderly father, but she came to accept that he was in good hands with her sister nearby. Perhaps most important, Maureen also had something to look forward to; she had long anticipated enjoying an outdoor recreational lifestyle in the mountains.

Externally, the changes in her practice wrought by government mandates and a new electronic medical records system caused her deep frustration, dissatisfaction, and even a pain in the neck. Another external factor was Maureen's daughter, whose decision to settle in Idaho reinforced Maureen's intention to leave Indiana and retire out West.

Chapter 14
Frank's Story

Frank is an 81-year-old gentleman who started his accounting firm in 1963. Though still in the midst of making his retirement decision, I've included his story in this book because Frank and his wife are a charming couple who went out of their way to speak with me. I met with Frank and his wife together. Although I asked Frank the same questions as other interviewees in this book, in many instances they replied as a couple and so his story is presented in a slightly different format.

When Frank was in his 50's, two major clients moved their operations to another region and took their business with them. Frank noted, "I was too young to retire, but I knew it was going to be difficult to replace that business." At that time, his conception of retirement was "sitting at home, maybe playing some golf". Having seen friends wither under such circumstances he wanted nothing of it, and yet he realized that remaining in the Midwest was increasingly unappealing both professionally and personally, especially in the winter. He and his wife decided to relocate to Miami where their son had established a branch office of their firm. Frank maintained his Midwest office, shuttling back and forth to serve existing clients while helping to build up a book of business in Florida.

In the past few years, his wife encouraged him to slow down. Frank had resisted, saying,

> "I've always been active; I don't like
> to sit still. When she says slow down,
> I reply *look at others my age who
> haven't slowed down!* I don't want
> my mind to atrophy. For 50 years I've
> gone to the office every day."

Frank's son too wanted him cut back a bit, feeling that there was simply no need for him to work so hard. He encouraged his father to take his foot off the throttle, and three weeks prior to our interview Frank agreed to take off every Friday.

This shift in his schedule also coincided with a major change in his living situation. Frank and his wife had been living in a large home that required substantial upkeep. For years his wife had wanted to downsize and she finally convinced him to move to a smaller home in an active senior living community. So on his first two Fridays off, he spent his day preparing and staging his home for sale.

Frank said that his degree of comfort with taking Fridays off would depend on whether he can find enjoyable ways to occupy his time. He was optimistic because his new community offers a huge range of activities and amenities. I asked him whether he would consider taking even more days off per week. He replied, "I really like what I'm doing. Even if there are other interesting activities available in our community, I don't feel I'd be missing anything by being at work."

Frank acknowledged that a time might come when he would need to scale back further. "I hope that I'll have enough sense to know that something is wrong. Perhaps if I'm not absorbing things, then I should stop working. I hope that my son will tell me."

Frank's advice for people thinking of retiring:

"As long as you feel well, keep active. Don't just stop. Don't divorce yourself from everything."

Observations about Frank's retirement decision

Frank's decision-making process is incremental. Some might argue that he hasn't really decided to retire at all. He simply shifted to a four-day workweek, and it doesn't sound as if he is inclined to take further steps any time soon.

Right now Frank is adjusting to two major changes simultaneously. Perhaps the change in his living situation impacts his views about retiring. Once he grows more comfortable with his new home, he might be more open to considering further modifications to his work schedule.

I wasn't able to explore why Frank finally agreed to a four-day workweek. I suspect it was the most palatable option for him at that moment. It keeps him in the game, it keeps his wife and son happy, and it gives him more flexibility with regard to how he thinks of himself (and presents himself to others). If neighbors in his new community ask him about himself, he can either say that he is still working or semi-retired, and both statements would be true.

Chapter 15
Conclusions

These stories reflect the experiences of a tiny percentage of those grappling with the decision to retire. Though small in number, the individuals interviewed for this book have shared a glimpse into the many considerations that influenced their decision making process.

Virtually all of my respondents reported at least one significant *external* factor that contributed to their decision. These included things like new corporate owners, a shift in the marketplace, and/or disruptive technological developments. For example, Ray, Walter and Brian all found themselves working for new bosses they didn't care for. Henry and Maureen commented that government mandates were increasingly impacting their work. The mental health center where Beverly practiced lost its funding. Nathan saw that his younger colleagues had cutting edge skills that would carry the practice into the future.

Other external factors include Ben's observation that he wasn't getting many assignments. Leslie's business partner set an example for her by announcing his own retirement date. Sharon reached the age when she could take advantage of the phased step-down arrangement offered by her firm. Arthur's son told him in no uncertain terms that he needed to relinquish his leadership role.

Equally compelling were the *internal* psychological factors that my respondents reported. Some of these were predominantly negative. Leslie found herself growing emotionally weary from demanding clients and the stress of managing production facilities in Mexico. Henry became increasingly unable to tolerate his back pain. Nathan started to lose confidence in his surgical skills. Ray acknowledged the reality that his cancer treatment impacted his performance. Walter no longer felt a sense of autonomy at work.

On the other hand, some of the internal factors were essentially positive. Sharon reached a point where she found herself ready to make a change and have more fun. Brian's counselor helped him reflect upon his accomplishments and conclude that he had achieved what was most important to him. Charles grew hopeful about his post-work life after discussing retirement with a friend. Maureen became confident that her father was in good hands with her sister nearby. Arthur recognized that he must not create the same discord with his son that he encountered with his own father.

For many of my respondents there was a *convergence* of internal <u>and</u> external factors that led to their decision to retire. It was as if their psychological readiness *coincided* with external circumstance. I believe that when the emotional factors are in sync with situational factors it makes the decision process easier.

Conversely, I suspect that when internal and external factors are not aligned the decision may be more fraught. Imagine someone who is ready to retire psychologically, but the external circumstances don't support that step. For example, Sharon's decision might have been much harder if her law firm didn't offer phased retirement, or if her husband intended to continue working full time. Conversely, there are times when external circumstances mandate retirement even though the person is not psychologically ready. For example, had Arthur done more emotional preparation he might have been far more comfortable stepping aside and letting his son take over the company.

What about people like Frank who aren't really contemplating retiring? According to a 2014 Gallup poll, 10% of baby boomers said they had no plans to retire. I've met many of these "retirement resisters" over the years and they often proudly declare their intention to work indefinitely. On the one hand I admire their resolve, yet some of their proclamations could arguably be met with a question . . .

Proclamation	Question
"I'm never going to retire"	How do you know that's in the best interests of your business and your family?
"I'm having too much fun to stop"	Did you ever hear this piece of advice about parties: "Always leave while you're still having a good time!"

"They'll have to wheel me out of here on a stretcher"	What impact might that have on your company and your clients?
"I intend to die at my desk"	Is that the BEST you can do with your wisdom and experience? *

* with thanks to my colleague Paul Cronin at *The Platinum Years*.

I suppose one could hypothesize that deep down these people might be grappling with any number of emotional obstacles to retirement such as:

- I'm afraid I'll be irrelevant.
- I'm afraid of getting older.
- I'm afraid I'll get sick like my mother or father did once they retired.
- I'm afraid I'll run out of money.
- I'm afraid I'll be bored.
- I'm afraid it will be uncomfortable spending so much time with my spouse.

LARRY GARD

But the fact is, I hear these exact same anxieties from my clients who are *actively planning* their retirement. We heard them from many of the respondents in this book. Therefore I'm not convinced that fear is what's driving those who intend to work forever. I'd like to propose an alternative explanation:

They have not yet discovered a more compelling alternative to working full time.

Here are a few possible reasons why:

They didn't have sufficient time to develop meaningful, truly gratifying avocations.

Some people were fully immersed in their business or career, either by choice or by necessity, leaving little opportunity to cultivate other interests.

They never had a role model.

Many people grew up with parents who worked until they could no longer do so, and consequently they had no role model of someone who enjoyed an active and rewarding retirement.

They feel uncomfortable not working.

Baby boomers tend to have a strong work ethic. A willingness to put in long hours and get the job done is admirable and can serve us well. Unfortunately some people overuse this strength to the point that they feel ill at ease when they're not working.

Telling these individuals to "stop working so hard" and "take time for themselves" is ineffective. Many people are justifiably irritated by such unsolicited advice. I have many close friends who insist that it's their prerogative to work as long as they please. I'm inclined to agree, as long as they recognize the impact of doing so on all the stakeholders involved.

So how should we respond to those who say they'll never retire? We owe them respect for their experience, tenacity, and accomplishments. We also owe them honest feedback if their work is doing more harm than good. And if we perceive an opening, we can help them discover compelling alternatives to full time employment.

After a lifetime of satisfying work, what could be better? My respondents would probably reply, "lots of things - but unless you plan for them and look for them, you may not see them." Many had some idea of what they wanted their retirement to look and feel like, even if they didn't have a detailed plan for making it so. They had something in mind that was drawing them toward the future.

Charles and Maureen looked forward to moving out West to hike and ski. Nathan hoped to travel, sail, and play golf. Beverly wanted to combine seeing clients with travel and coursework. Brian anticipated tackling home projects and entertaining friends. Leslie contemplated pursuing a Ph.D. in Economics. Henry and his wife imagined enjoying hobbies and cultural interests. Sharon viewed retirement as an opportunity to be more spontaneous and spend more time with her grandchild. Ben and his wife sought to have an active, urban lifestyle.

For readers facing their own retirement decision, the stories presented here raise multiple questions:

1. What external factors are leading you to consider retirement?

2. What internal factors are leading you to consider retirement?

3. To what extent are the external and internal factors converging?

4. To what extent are your beliefs and assumptions about retirement driven by what you saw happen to parents and grand-parents?

5. What alternative(s) to working full time might appeal to you?

I hope that as you give thought to these questions and reflect on the stories in this book, your decision will come more easily to you. I'm pleased to report that many of my respondents spontaneously remarked that they found the interview process thought provoking and emotionally satisfying. Their positive reaction speaks to the complexity of the retirement decision and the benefit of having in-depth conversations about it.

If such a discussion is helpful after the fact (as my interviewees reported) imagine how useful it might be well in advance of your retirement. To find trained professionals who can assist you in examining the head and heart aspects of this transition, visit:

The Platinum Years
(https://www.theplatinumyears.com/find-advisors/)

or

The American Psychological Association
(http://locator.apa.org/)

ABOUT THE AUTHOR

Larry Gard is a psychologist and principal of Hamilton-Chase Consulting in Chicago. His doctoral training at Northwestern University Medical School focused on the second half of life. He helps clients sort through the complex issues related to the sale of a business and/or retirement, while overcoming emotional barriers that prevent planning for the future. Larry can be reached at **drlgard@hamiltonchaseconsulting.com**.

For more information about this book and other programs related to retirement, please visit

www.donewithwork.org

Made in the USA
Columbia, SC
24 June 2019